Roundabout

Also by Roger Furphy

Fiction
Two Brothers (Primavera Press, 1996)
Mainly Manly (Jacoan Press, 1998)

Poetry
Footsteps Passing (2001)
Moments Passing (2003)
A Morning Compass (2007)
Roaming (Ginninderra Press, 2013)

Roger Furphy

Roundabout

Roundabout
ISBN 978 1 76109 622 8
Copyright © text Roger Furphy 2023
Cover image: Polina Kovaleva from Pexels

First published 2023 by
GINNINDERRA PRESS
PO Box 3461 Port Adelaide 5015
www.ginninderrapress.com.au

Contents

Roundabout	11
About family	
A daughter	15
'And anyway'	16
Annie	17
Crossover	18
Fifty Years On	19
Grandchildren	20
Her iPad	21
Round about this land	
Alice Springs	25
Australian Open	26
Autumn Sun – Yarra Valley	27
Barwon Bridge	28
Beach Lullaby	29
Block Arcade	30
Broken Hill	31
Changing Farms	32
Clouds over Barwon	33
Doors closing	34
East West	37
From a Bus	38
From Little River Railway Station	39
House on the Hill	40
Melbourne Trams	41
Merimbula	42
Murray River	43
Noosa (Years on)	44
Numbers that name a street	45

Once	46
Oodnadatta Track	47
Robe	48
Sounds of a beach	50
South Australian Eucalyptus	51
Tarneit Railway Station	52
Tea Tree	53
The boab	54
The Boobialla	55
The Ghan Then and Now	56
The Kurrajong Hotel	57
The Rockford Winery	58
Thylacine and Stripes Around	59
Waves	60
Waves	61
Waves	62

About other places

America – 'Oh America'	65
Bridges Apart	67
Notre Dame	68
Obama Returned	70
Oh, come to me Tuscany	71
Trumped	72
Tuscany Visited	73
Webb's space	74

Roundabout

Are we there yet?	77
Back-packed	78
Best Protest	79
Bubbles	80
Butterfly	81

Connecting Waters	82
Covid 19 (expelling form)	83
Degustation	84
Directional Dots	85
Dry Red	86
Francesca	87
French Rhythm	89
Hail	90
Hans Heysen	91
Overkill	92
Overpassed	93
Reading at Readings	94
Roadkill	95
Roundabout of dreams	96
Searching paddocks	97
Small shelters	98
Smart Retro Bistro	99
The Batsman and the Butterfly	100
Yesterday's news	102
The potter and the moulder	103
The Pull	104
The seatbelt	106
The Sideways Kick	107
Urban Highs and Lows	108
Van Gogh Exhibition	109
Words Meeting	110
Writers Festival, Adelaide 2018	111
Yesterday's cars	112

About this ageing vessel

Administration and Admission	115
Any time soon	116

Floors	117
Foghorn and Ultrasound	118
Footsteps	119
In Confined Urgency	120
It's Inconclusive	121
Night Decks	122
Night passage	123
Old Shadows	124
Red	125
The Curtain Pull	126
The Food Tray	127
Acknowledgements	128
About the Author	129

'The greatest imperfection is in our inward sight, that is, to be ghosts unto our own eyes.'
– *Christian Morals* (1716) part 3, section 15
Sir Thomas Browne

Roundabout

circles, swirls direction, contemplates
        exit of story line
and where they might lead
    of distance between
the curve of metaphor that loops
      hesitation of progress
a side road as diversion that peters
        to a deaden end
these poems take the short cut the
          back roads of distant between
in a roundabout sort of way

About family

A daughter

a daughter
calm in the resting wards
        of maternity

and her daughter
swaddled in wrap

the telepathy between
the instinct of bond

day old and already
talking in tongues
empathy from a wash
        of pleasanter

new life
in a swell of love

'And anyway'

as a flywheel
evolving her conversation
    rolling her story
till intermittent the double-click of cam
registers different direction
her hesitation of humdrum
clicks in, 'and anyway',
the story rolls on
as sheets before print
words form as leaves falling
    'and anyway'
or a chance of interruption
'and anyway,' it's notice of continuation
revolving resolve, going either way…
or anyway,
but anyway,
    let's continue.

Annie

she came to a world
washed on waves of joy,
beached on the grey soils
of a Wimmera inland,
then roamed in hunter shoals
        of schoolgirl desire
dropped anchor in channels north
the drop-bars and waterwheels
churning a valley, bearing fruit
        all on an incoming tide,
and now there's ebb in her flow
        sand dunes away
down Point Lonsdale way,
receding from the high and low
        of a city's pull,
to smooth sands washed
    in tide's memory
the drum of surf at night
beating a rhythm to new dreams
        cleansing the old,
and morning birds calling
        seasons' harmony
as a piano distant, reading her notes.

Crossover

there was a crossover between us
me on the Hume, northbound
tracking home to visit him
such the urgency of
        late cancer calls,
and overhead
a helicopter throbbing its beat southwards
and unbeknown, a brother outstretched
air-ambulanced, churning operational
to operation
and my thoughts clustered to our family
of siblings
him 60 now and me 14 years older
and those in between
my teenage years and mum still
        breastfeeding him
this baby that would grow taller than us,
challenge the conventions of
our conservative world,
fight this blossom of cancer
stem its rampant growth,

and now this crossover
still miles apart
but somehow closer

Fifty Years On

she came to Shepp on January winds
warmed by north and west
and somehow to me she stood out
from the rest

fifty years, cheers!

her small white mini
and from open front door
unfolding long legs
and my mates all turned their heads

fifty years, cheers!

then the joy of children of horses and dog
but never a cat
and up in the hills our stone-walled shack.

fifty years, ah my dear, cheers!

and now there's grandchildren
with us tonight
we think of them most days
in early morning light.

fifty years, my everlasting love, cheers!

Grandchildren

(interstate)

they holiday their lope to me
arms extended and smile
that creases a telepathy
            of heredity
they have grown shouldering
backpack and independence
        within
from airports short journey
        domestic
soon to grow the international routes
leaving our hearts behind

Her iPad

before there were books
to take her away from him,
his food, his lumps of washing,
his television squared and cornered,
his toenails clicked onto faded red rug,
both now washed away from the tumble of life
pages turned to predictable outcome
till now, and an iPad connecting her again
photos through clouds, bring grandchildren
hanging around, yet spaced

Round about this land

Alice Springs

as a book opening between ranges
turning to open its spine of River Todd
and page either side
records of explorers, police, a telegraph line
of past and present, of air conditioning,
super malls and galleries

alas some pages remain shut
from the hinge of centre
in hidden guilt
those camped in river's bed
boozed by an intoxicated moon
unable to turn an earmarked page
to move to a next chapter

Australian Open

yesterday's colosseum without the bones of column
the stone arches and shadows beyond,
now billboards of information and lenses honing in,
seating us as keyboard dots in rows of letters and number
its dome hunch of roof that opens to sky
exhaling echo the tapered grunt of endeavour,
and the rallies end of cheer, of Aussie, Aussie, Aussie.

breaths in silence, the bounce of ball before the serve
the squeak of shoe holding ground from foot fault,
until the end,
as gladiators once did separated by stone plinth
their balls and chain,
they come to the net that crossed them,
double-faulted them, before the handshake.

Autumn Sun – Yarra Valley

light fades a day
as metabolism arranges our seasons
time zones our interchange within
blinks a slow setting
sinking on blanket clouds

autumn sun dresses colour of leaf
on vineyards chorus line
razes a side of hill then falls down the other
dabs impressionist dots on sun-dried flora
winds the pendulum of our footstep,
shorter now, in autumn light.

Barwon Bridge

doubles us over and back
on tide's rise and fall
shares double crossover
and parallel return
frames motion through rails
clicks static shutter of reflection
on mirror blue
on ocean's side dunes slope
to a river's mouth and beyond
a slow formation of waves builds
to splash their entrance
sand harbours build up one side
muscle in as nature does
upstream, sandbars bare slender skins
on current's tidal pull
across, a village its roundabout to all traffic
and a supermarket
not super big

Beach Lullaby

oh, come to me – down to the sea
its depth's dark reach – that shallows to beach

oh, come to me – the waves of the sea
their contoured roll – as Neptune's scrolls
their laugh of white splash – the sound of their crash

oh, come to me – the gulls on the beach
and those further out – gliding their reach
oh, come to me
the hooded plover – away from dunes' cover
its scratch on the sand – as shorthand scanned

oh, come to me – the sound of night seas
the torment of waves folding away
oh, come to me – the throb of diesels' purr
and pilot boat's engine up and down whirr

oh, come to me – a ship's forward wedge
its cargo stacked high – as it enters the heads

oh, come to me.

Block Arcade

from Collins Street, arched arcade,
its forged bangles of iron scribble filigree
step on a wash of terrazzo as coins splashed
old skins of brass frame small shops coveting possession
cloths of Milan, leather of Venice, shoes from Italy,
a crush of table and chair sidesteps direction
lingers intake of coffee aroma
till drunken in contemplation,
the ambience of this place.

Broken Hill

flat top ridges as a table bare
silver gone missing,
washed down the phosphorus,
sulphide and chlorine streets
from the fibro and corrugation
of miners' homes,
the perpetual smile of garden gnomes
stranded on front yard's red earth,
waving memory of those moved on
but forever lasting as stone buildings
downtown

Changing Farms

changing farms once small farms squatted from walls of hillside
stone fences squared to ten-acre boundaries
hemmed fabric patchwork over spreading fields
dabbed dots of geranium around stone cottage
a tank stand flared in dresses of bougainvillea

animals content under a drowsy sky

until the multiply of takeover stretches distance
sheds harbour machinery waiting in idle anticipation
their headlights that will harvest night skies
the comb of cutting edge in one-sided spread
a hunger to gulp summer's wave of sunflower
to gorge the gluten succulent of headed wheat
the molten splendour of barley, the oils of canola.

Clouds over Barwon

the accumulation of cumulus
floats on warm western winds
as if squeezed from the corrugated
openings of Western District
woolsheds
before the pressing
from oily floors and the table
of wool classers
to form as mobs again,
floating above the confines of fencing
drifting east along a coastline
to sunset's colours
sheeted to knitted strata
of mauves and pinks
till resting in night's darkness
on the undulation of Barwon Heads fairways
till sunrise and reformed to fairways' contour
they lift on morning breezes
coloured in the dusty reds of sunrise
from where they grew.
and gathered in western skies
as mid-morning flocks in misty fog
that will lose the golf ball from tee
darken their intent before raining
a downpour of revenge,
crack a whiplash of lightning,
muffle the bark of thunder
one thousand sheepdogs strong,
not satisfied until the bleat of siren
that will drive members up clubhouse ramps
to their roomy pens.

Doors closing

Sydney's Central to Pymble stations

Central Station –   walkways reach as tentacles
              circle to exit and entry
              its caterpillar spine of escalator
              and nodular calm of those
              carried to platforms below
              'Doors closing' –'Please stand clear'

Town Hall Station –   its rush of dark air in cellar warmth
              echoes those in catacomb of routine
              the fluorescent X-ray of torsos in motion
              'Doors closing' – 'Please stand clear'

Wynyard Station –   last before the bridge and
              suddenly afternoon sun through
              the crisscross of a Meccano arch
              frames white splashes of wave
              on blue waters below
              'Doors closing' – 'Please stand clear'

Milson Point Station – elevated from roads around
              steps down to Luna Park,
              its smiling face swallowing
              jelly bean kids through
              'Doors closing' – 'Please stand clear'

North Sydney –   suddenly fashion steps from trains
              as moths floating on summer air
              their glide to apartments
              or contemporary boxed architecture of office
              'Doors closing' – 'Please stand clear'

Waverton Station –	from platform on high-rise
	and tunnels that blink darkness to light
	camellias squat tubbed as stamps
	the length of platform's envelope.
	'Doors closing' – 'Please stand clear'
Wollstonecraft Station –	there's a train here, the other way
	resting, breathing air
	compressed, then exhaling
	'Doors closing' – 'Please stand clear'
St Leonards Station –	cutting in, leaning walls of clay
	ochre seams as indigenous graffiti
	veins of white ridge as dinosaurs' bone
	'Doors closing' – 'Please stand clear'
Artarmon Station –	over freeways swath, suburban eucalypts
	reach through dollops of light
	occasional shafts spotlight
	a dog on lead along leafy path
	'Doors closing' – 'Please stand clear'
Chatswood Station –	a splash of graffiti as Thai art
	perhaps mandarin hieroglyphic
	designer bags bulging designer logo
	tempting 'Westfield', the expectation of 'chatty'
	or a golden Peking duck extended neck and leg
	displayed from gallows of shop front window,
	'Doors closing' – 'Please stand clear'

Roseville Station –   camellia, azalea, geranium,
in old English ambience, as a table set
the silver of carriage as cutlery set
before moving,
'Doors closing' – 'Please stand clear'

Lindfield Station –   from platform up steps to walkway each way
above the line in misty rain, fog,
and memory of steam trains going under.
'Doors closing' – 'Please stand clear'

Gordon Station –   schools around uniform them
gathers their swarming parade
from platform's reach,
stretches them to small groups
mirrors their extended confidences
from windows passing reflection
'Doors closing' – 'Please stand clear'

Pymble Station –   doors open to familiar platform,
past its bulge of ticket machine,
along its yellow ridges of plastic dots
distant highway traffic drones backdrop
to a final exhausted sigh,
'Doors closing' – 'Please stand clear'

East West

Merimbula – Pambula – Tathra – Narooma
Tilba Tilba. 'Ah! All the "a" endings.'
'Ah, but remember the "up"s over west',
Kooranup – Jardinup – Muranup – Mandinup.
so could it be one might ask
that twin latitudes, and distance between
have forced a difference, a them and us?
a decline in attitudes that we might call
across the deserts between,
'ah' – 'up' – 'you too.'

From a Bus

Fleurieu Peninsula

winding down bald hills, a coast
its ripple of blue chenille,
unbuttoned the red dome of sunset,
undressing a night sky
slipping through the hems of light and dark,

and those hills up there,
their crease of valley turning them round,
stripped to bare skins
as buttocks and bosoms
their slope of shoulder nudging
caress on their sheets of history.

From Little River Railway Station

to the west 'You Yangs' lay
as if pre-volcanic
and a little river winding down
as unsevered umbilical
asleep in time's interruption
nesting Barwon prison beside
and prisoners wombed in waiting
locked in a confinement of conformity
the distant sound of traffic
and a fast train screaming
commuters' freedom
from Geelong to Southern Cross Station

House on the Hill

the house on the hill and near a sea
winks veranda lights to ships
passing in twilight's breeze

and in winter morning's fog
distant a lighthouse drawl
of foghorn
its stutter of intermittent stall
and cattle on the hill their plaintiff recall

and horses once stabled here
stamp on earthen floor
before next morning's polo cheer

and an oval green confining a team
poised in flannels stretching seam

rooms off a passage wide and long
open and shut doors
generations of steps prolonged

and from a back door a vestibule square
where workmen removed boots
and aprons hung there

and down a hill, a train line
parallel entwined
its memory of puffed smoke behind

and in hot summer breeze
on a January night
there's entertainment here
to everyone's delight

Melbourne Trams

there's sway causing shoulders' touch
Melbourne trams teasing season's momentum
framed through window passing
spring winds toss elms together
the shimmer of young leaf as lips kissing
until the mechanics of peak hour
that will corral our rigid stand
and next stop that will jam us
full body
tempting awkward smiles

Merimbula

lakes breathe their tides on
        mudflat skins
wallow on earth's time frame
soak reflected sun by day
drink the moon as red wine by night

ignore the glint of apartment
the highway bridging a gap
the hybrid shooting star of Jetstar

remember instead the pearl white
        of midden's shells
the loop of melaleuca trees as
        music written
the slope of rock as outposts, guarding

Murray River

and now it runs full
bloated from the excesses
    of a climate changed,
swirls dimples of back water,
lifts on the banks of red gum,
slides a quick silver current
    of earthen colours,
broadens wide-eyed reflection,
of cormorant's bloated flight,
the glide of pelican before
        their skim on river,
spills from banks to billabongs
          and swamps,
their boudoirs of mirrors,
that will pamper complexions,
the pink of gums after shedded
        bark,
foliage brushed as hairstyles
        to drying winds,
enticing bullfrog their deep
          throated pursuit,
spills spoonfuls of moonlight
        as pearls resting,
splayed in floods of emotion

Noosa (Years on)

I had observed them, coupled
beached as old rocks
their tide coming, going out

their August northward to Noosa
degrees of twenty-four
and all those years between
back rested on antiquities
of folded chairs
and shaded only by conversation

slower now to ocean's edge
their step as water birds
swamped in slow contemplation

down in Pacific's rim
they wallow as kelps to and fro
from waves gentle pull and push

Numbers that name a street

Mildura's boulevards, its main road
    stretching west,
    and cross streets, from third to
    thirty-second street,
till out of town on orange trees' fringe

    was it those Californian boys?
    those Chaffey brothers?
    their rows of irrigation channels
    or pumps numbered in words,
    from second to twenty-fifth
    on every other deep river bend

was it their suggestion that streets
    be named in similar style?
    perhaps nostalgia for old
    New York,
or a local borough, chuffed
and grateful for a new prosperity,
abandoned their proposed
King, Queen and Princess streets

Once

Yorta Yorta on big river's bend
and now our towns in super mall trend,

Yorta Yorta art that hangs contemporary
yet in spiritual past,
the super mall selling things that won't last.

Yorta Yorta their camps on ochre clays,
the super mall, bitumen surrounds, melting on hot days.

Yorta Yorta on river bank sands
around a fire in circled crouch,
the super mall, with chairs and couch
and us in unhealthy lazy slouch.

Yorta Yorta, under shaded trees
a gentle sound through leaf's breeze,
the super mall, its conditioned air
silent, refrigerated,
and us,
in homogenised despair.

Oodnadatta Track

around the edge of desert's spread
the lap of Eyre's lake on mud-soaked sands
saddles ridges sparse in blue grey saltbush
corrugation jars the internals of car, and us,
the ramp ripples a shiver of elevation
and further out dunes parallel direction
as shoals through waves of time
reflect ochre shimmer red and blue
from desert's deserted time frame

Robe

foothills fade to coastal plains
then to sanctuaries of estuaries and bays
a reverence to motherland's waterways,

the umbilical severed at ocean's reach
and old man Murray finally beached,
its long wind of memory on currents flow
its level of highs and lows,
water pumped to higher dams
irrigated, spread to laser land,

inland, further, tracks etched by explorers reach,
gentry on horse and drays
to claim those northern plains,

and Chinese long walk
to avoid a colony's tax rort,
their sandals and wigwams
weighed down on stoic plan,
propelled by the nostril of dragons' steam
or so it all seemed –
to goldfields, their rush of dream,
later their woks and pans to small towns
communities embraced, satisfied
their hunger pangs

back in Robe, jewelled and robed
John Piggott, on emu's back
mounted small hills saddleback,
low sun's dim sheen on the silver of stirrup
holding leathers reach
and above its halter a revolver's breach,

the 'Birdman of Coorong' on emu's back
he'd hold up lone travellers on sandy tracks,
and they'd hunt him down – like Kelly they would
till finally from the Coorong, he was rid.

Sounds of a beach

the white break of wave suddenly ungloved
broken to a beach, fingers reach as drumsticks
                                        to incessant rattle
further out a knotted fist, the roll of shoulder
the pitch of elbow break booms base background
the cymbals of foam, effervescent in rise and fall
and upwind the orchestra of rhythm on waves roll
and yet more distant intermittent along keyboard
                                          of coastline
a seagulls' stanza call conducting a pleading rhythm

South Australian Eucalyptus

those gums, as armies holding their ground
others alone, in deep-rooted defiance
their mottled camouflage shedding bark
their memory of young men on horses
driving cattle through,
and those that didn't come back
reason too they hold their ground
that a spirit be shaded there, resting,
knowing that they too will lose limbs,
hollow out as those young Aussies did,
                    hanging on.

Tarneit Railway Station

west of Melbourne from
corridors of new housing
the quiet walk of refugees
up ramps and on board
indifferent to time's schedule
as if still drifting in boats
eyes wide to their slow search
of place
seated around us, between us,
or standing, their passages of time
calm in their momentum of sway,
and a train accelerating
till the moan of top gear
comes like whales calling
in the night

Tea Tree

its coastal cumulus blotches
the undulation of sand dunes
rolls reflected as clouds above,
weathers winter's wind
on knurled twists of branch
as old elbows resting on bars,
hoards a pattern of clover leaf
as daubs of impressionist art,
until spring winds whisper
sighs of content through,
pout kisses of flower cluster
           defiant
daring as sundresses on girls
before the long hot nights
           of summer

The boab

its golliwog reach
arms and hands scratching
                       the sky
its trunk bellied
goanna filled

along a highway
crossing the Fitzroy
its moon puddles

distant their stand
as fat ladies
beached on desert sands
crazed to maddening heat

The Boobialla

Myoporum Insulare

just weeks from Christmas
a stay of execution
reprieve from hard prune

unlike Christmas trees
propped on severed trunks
bunched as prostitutes for sale
on highway corners

the Boobialla reaches for space
on a Lonsdale street
extending over a warm blanket
of bitumen road
its British green foliage
our Australian holly
and now bursting small dots of flower
on winds of a thousand kisses.
its ribbon of flowers.

but old Roddy (up the road)
done with season's monotony
and tired of bending his morning walk
underneath
came armed with chain saw
before the Christmas rush
pruned hard its wrappings of green
its ribbon of flowers
his growl of song ('The Last Noel')
and exhaust of carbon
his incense of myrrh

The Ghan Then and Now

before the Ghan they were camel drivers
Middle Eastern Muslims peeling the edges
of desert life to distant outposts
their rugs at night to an eastern sky

now a new Ghan reaches north, south
stencils diesel stamp on parallel lines
and sleepers where dreaming clicks a rhythm
on flicker of mirage or imagination
and once the trail of camels across
another day

The Kurrajong Hotel
Canberra

an exodus expires a year
this week before Christmas,
politicians on earlier planes
staff and bureaucrats, last drinks,
at the Kurrajong Hotel
their corners of alcove
expanse of veranda and window slats
louvred in late afternoon sun
that sifted a year of conversation
before the public ear
young men and women
discreet to the power of others
the boxed departments and walks between
soon lonely in summer heat
to towns and cities they left behind
to their Christmas with parents
and families all so far away

The Rockford Winery

bald hills umbrella the winery
cellar its ambiance as old wines
cool stone walling us in
and doorways that bend us through
on hinges elbow turn
and bottles lined drinking in
the comment of critique,
the swirl of wine glass flashing
shades of light
as sundresses
in spring winds do

outside, grapes hand-picked
and shovelled to shoots
stripped to stem's waste
as a thousand hands severed
before fermentation sets in
a rhythm of progress and the tick
of timing cam on a Ronaldson
stationary engine
and flywheel with a hundred years of turn
a whir of leather belts and oiled shafts
through bearings and pumps
regurgitating a season's ripening

Thylacine and Stripes Around

broken from southern shores, non-conformed,
a patch torn from the cloth of Terra Australis
its label unstitched, 'Van Diemen's Land',
of Huon crashed in fallen rest
logs ended circling stripes around
before a mill that planked them
arched their ply from bow to stern

of aboriginal with ochre stripe full-blooded
and chains around that shackled them away

Thylacine, tiger-striped around lean hind flanks
and tapered tail that closes grasses behind,
his jaw set as trap around him
and still they see his flash across a paddock
his fluorescent stripes in headlights
they remember the 'last known in captivity'
his escape from a zoo
his dormant den of breeding as angels must do
until the next sighting

Waves

Impressionists that never stroked deep blue

just a coastline but never further out
of oceans deep, sinking skies horizon
far from the impressionist, landed on colours growth
of seasons change and lakes pooled reflection
and farmhouse in spotted domestication
of shade and light distant dobs
angled in mottles sameness
accentuating a moment's daylight

but out there deep fathoms reluctance
its blue of depth in manic toss of swell
trapped in shafts of depth, fighting release
to a shoreline

Waves

A seascape

closer in there is urgency to crest
to reach a starting line before break
build condition on offshore winds
foam crests on mists of salt
before crash to a beach
the linger of orgasm up skins
of beaches smooth contour

Waves

To an audience beached

long legs of wave in distant taper
growing formation shaping choreography
and in between sloshing hollow resistance
shallow the rise to beaches stage
the advance of orchestral finale
graduated volume before curtain's call
the boom of base, the flute as seagulls lifting
the violin shouldering arms in hesitant hold
symbols, tingle n foaming fade
curl a chorus line in daring break
fades on the rise of beaches effervescent

About other places

America – 'Oh America'

1955
Gary Cooper walked High at Noon
across a world of cinema screen
down a dusty western street
tall lean
           leathers
bowed to the round of horse
           steps
short in frames of contemplation
slow his southern drawl,

'Do not forsake me, Oh my darling'
(to draw and shoot, one on one)
'On this our wedding day'

and it seemed OK,
'Oh, how I loved America'

fifty years on
George Bush sways approach
to a western media
stuffed, his swagger
arms wide from invisible holster,

to draw on some phrases
           to unload leaden wisdom

'we're goin' ta stay on'…
'we're goin' ta see it through'…
'this is a war on terror'…

and most citizens here and there
nod heads on jelly shoulders

'Oh, how I despise America'

Bridges Apart

Paris bridges leave memory locked on
scan the years between divided
singles until the hoop of lock couples them
clicked in security hold and keys thrown over
their mark of Napoleonic chivalry
vowing one day to return, their honest intent.
till away from the sigh of Seine, to hometown chatter
and what they might know, and what they might do,
and what they might say, and what they might say
one day.

Notre Dame

from the Seine its traffic
of river cruise tourists nested roof top
of barges joined slewing their load,
Ponts across a left and right bank
over currents of springs season change
the seasons of easter
and the week before resurrection,
Parisians on Pont des Arts in late afternoon sun
their disbelief and prayer and cluster of choir
as distant birds call over water,
Notre Dame in flames on its altar of isle

since thirteenth century its smoulder of incense
wafted layers of caress on internal walls
mellow aged sheen on sculptured stature
perfumed musk crowded portraits
and powdered rotund infant angels,
ignited now and into the night
a devil flame
stoked by centuries of aged oak
their forest of beams, its kindle
of gothic spire that would arch
slow-motion fall
sheeted lead melted to silver beads
fallen as a thousand rosaries spread,
yet the miracle of daybreak its promised light
the dome of bell towers, stone walls and turrets
standing defiant
the gargoyle's slight expression of smile
and medieval stained windows somehow
winked their colours through,

Popes from Avignon once pilgrimed here,
Napoleon from his white steed tethered
       crowned emperor here,
millions hobbled on cobblestone
    to worship here,
and President Macron declared, France
will rebuild Notre Dame again.

Obama Returned

until a first debate
his lope of speech
stepping us through
as his African brothers
their long distant stride
to an Olympic end
a monologue tribal
ripening republicans' concern
the red of Michelle's dress
and her all-American man
until the blue and red corners
of Ohio and Kentucky
Obama as the clay of Cassius
his long slow punchline
his sidestep left unsaid

until a victory speech
the mix of Afro-American smile
as so many cotton balls
in baskets on long backs
now his family on stage
a speech to all Americans

'Our American family, we rise and fall
over every hill, through every valley,
you lifted me up, I will not let you down.
I have listened to you, have learned from you.
more than a collection of red and blue space,
we are united
the United States of America.'

Oh, come to me Tuscany

oh, come to me, low hills of Tuscany
a roll over colour, harmony as no other.

oh, come to me, seated in threes
the wind of small road, the bus and its load.

oh, come to me, village Montalcino,
and us bouncing around, like happy bambino.

oh, come to me, the cypress so straight
as armies marching monotonous gait.

oh, come to me, the long light of day
that draws out expression
and what we might say,
and what we might see,
and what we might say

oh, come to me.

Trumped

his hair in a wave of vanity,
then his pout, mouthed
as fish food intake,
before the bubbles,
effervescent expletive
come breaking surface
exploding repeats that vanish
in uncoordinated release,
'Make America great again' and again,
'Tremendous' and again,
'Magnificent' twice, and again,
'Fake news' multiplied,
'Bad, very bad, very very bad' and again.
and tweets of short announcement
small words broken as children
reading from a picture book page.

Oh America! Oh America?

Tuscany Visited

oh, walk the hills of Tuscany
the slope of contoured colour,
leave footprint stamped to rich soils,
sit around stone habitat of yesteryear,
the farm dog that barks our wayward mob
the pines that pencil in boundaries
rest as brushes on easel's daub of colour,
the roof tops tucked in, with blankets of terracotta,
the village shops, small doors to small rooms
of crowded display,
and before sleep,
the rolling sweep of vista
that overcomes.

Webb's space

Hubble, now humbled in tumble
                to spaces reach
its telescopic probe that circles us
enlarged our universe of fading stars
our dimension beyond night's darkness
our yearning of exploration as once
                the earth was flat
now Webb casts its frame of lenses
astrophysicists focus a mesh of galaxies
stretching magnify light years away
shedding rocket skins discarded to
                other orbits
reaching other planets beyond moons
            pull of universal tides
unfolds giant shades as butterfly wings
                in dinosaurs glide
angled mirrors probe infrared lenses
            searching living growth
through haze of clustered milky way
storks deep shadows as night mountains
                in stagnant drift
their black hollow of universal edge
infinite space that taunts our dreams
            light years away

Roundabout

Are we there yet?

'are we there yet'
are we cruising with others?
are we careful on life's corners?
'are we there yet'
are we aware the uphills and downhills?
are we allowing space with others?
'are we there yet'

Back-packed

jet stream backpacks them down
southern crossed to a Golden Valley
lured to its ripening reach
their Euro lilt spoken through
        orchards' blush
late afternoon heat exhausts a day
till combi vans circle urban lake
open dusty doors in evening laugh
rest youthful limbs to branches
        of conversation
until season's end nomadic to inland tracks
the ripple of desert, escarpment of gorge
hanging ochre colour layered
as ripening fruit a handful of memory

    *

boats drifted them south
others on stamped refuge approval
pencil black their hyphenation between sentence
our question mark hooked to political word
        our hidden guilt
on summer evenings around urban lake
they group on grassed overlay
etching in, their rhythm of new life,
teenage youth loop circles of dance
        whistle their step
others sit rounded, secure
lost in memory of family
trapped in the huddle of war,
only the shriek of corellas, the calls of children,
remind them of now.

Best Protest

the best protest comes
surely by words alone
spoken, whispered, or shouted
in metaphorical tone

remember, 'I have a dream'
or 'How dare you', or
'Well may we say God save the Queen'.

so march your words
rally your message in chant
with contemplated lilt
rather than rant,

progress life's road of procession,
your words in gentle progression,
not smash and break
or disrupt with never a pause,
for surely then soon,
you will lose your cause.

Bubbles

those bubbles we blew,
our generation their wonder
          of multiple,
lifting floatation on transparent
          fragility,
a breeze that will twist shape
on elasticity of varied size,
drift as butterfly its direction
on the whim of autumn's hot winds.

most will burst in atmosphere's
          push and pull
crash a wall or bush at garden's edge
others a metre and a half away,
          then closer
clapped between tiny hands.

and years on, Covid 19, a virus
    that will chase us down
invisible, airborne, its globule spray
hidden bubbles floating his way,
knurled and knuckled hands
    in arthritic acceptance
to wash in soapy water (they say)
memories of dipping a bubble ring in,
a gentle blow of expectation
and bubbles drifting his world.

Butterfly

1

a butterfly tumbles spring winds
direction that loops continued return
celebration from its concertina of
caterpillar
and from a deck grounded
the old man, his spring sprung,
a butterfly flutters his contemplation
his straight line through all seasons
a beginning and an end
his chances of floating life's currents
missed

2

sun dresses her bare shoulders
and arms conducting rhythm
as floating a crest of body's wave
in synchronised strength
that touches suggestion
the flair of dress's edge
a butterfly at her shoulder
an angel in life's heaven
mirrors her movement
the pause, the lift on kisses
of breath
the turn that swishes a silence
waiting the moment

Connecting Waters

reflections come bold, moonscaped,
their ancestors' currents sweeping times bend,
their backwaters of contemplation that swirl
deep legends of mystery,
the snag of logs down from rivers edge
where once they reached spear to rivers wide,
from river gums till dots fade to desert grass
the emu the kangaroo stretched in probing gait,

and now on urban mass, a concrete spill,
a sculptured skate park contemporary
indigenous its swirls and bends,
and aboriginal youth ride on waves of heredity
silent their hover before launch, balanced direction
as forebears, their canoes in river currents
sharing a nation's platform, connecting waters.

Covid 19 (expelling form)

visualise a transparency of hidden form
globules holding our capsule of spray
                        enveloping,
exploding birth as first breath
no purpose but holding multiply
not a cell but a quantum within
sliding a sliver on lungs' sway
pumping till primed release,
to spread a world on sleeves of
                  humanity,
on the exhale of exchange
the air-conditioned carriage of travel,
holding magnetic determination
on all we touch and all we say,
its evaporated wetness as hail
                      melted
harmless its afterlife washed
                            in memory.

Degustation

around a degustation seated now in expectation
and a table laid bare from preparation
waiters stand by before their persuasion
eight courses prepared from kitchens' regurgitation
and in between evaluation
last course now in hesitant procrastination
the truffle and mushroom prawn
a revelation,
before that heavy feel of intergestation.

Directional Dots

they stop our step at corner kerb
their conveyer of colour to the sole of adidas
caressed by the soft pad of derelict's shuffle
a platform's edge parades them
as army in formation
protecting the gap between lines
our step back as train rushes in
the reds, yellows, and blues
as orchard's rows of fruit,
as jelly beans spilt, flattened on footsteps rush,
bright on the horizon of dull days
they lighten my step

Dry Red

speaking aesthetically

not pinot noir, its oxygen red as blood of newborn
    its grapes in premature round plucked as small
        handfuls of nursery
    resting sunbeam shafts through glass
        of early morning light

nor cabernet sauvignon and claret, as old girls
        dressed up
    their perfumes of blackberry – of liquorice –
        or the musk of old cloth
    their lipstick thick in dark reds
    and men that will read their labels
    of grapes from regions' rich soils
    bloated to seasons' excesses

nor the merlots and shiraz, aged as velvet curtains
    heavy in pleated tongues savouring
    the folds of winter warmth till dreams kick in

nor rosés, as the skins of young girls
    plucked before the heavy hand
    of tannins that slow ripening
        intoxicating life's desires.

ah, but dry red, its vines climbing hill's ridge
    rooted in stony shale that will work its thirst
    and grapes that hold their flush of colour
        through seasons' extremes
    and wine that quaffs working flavours
    that swills light laughs of moderation
    dances pirouettes that linger then fade.

Francesca

    in mounting yard's tight circle
    racehorses parade serene acceptance
        of what's to come,
there's rhythm here, the hollow ring
of anvil shoes on asphalt pavement,
the strapper reaching short to a bridle
        for those with temperament,
    longer on rein for others their
    nonchalant melancholy to the stare
        of punters' inspection,
    aware of their grooming
    the catwalk spring in their step
    the TV cameras zooming in
    and a moment with Francesca
    her catch up stride until instep
a similar gait now beauty and beast
and her Englishness of description
of mares, stallions, geldings, and maiden runs,
and her sun dress coloured to mock
the diamond and square carnival of
        puppet jockeys
her hair rolled as stored main, untouched
unpatable beneath small saddle of fascinator
    there's a trace of bridle too, that lingers
        her neckline that audios her word
her description of anatomy as only lovers could,
the flank, the rump, the stride, the temperament
and long neck that may just stretch to a line,
and as jockeys spring aboard, lifted by trainers
        and the big hearts of owners,

they circle once then head for the course,
my eyes are still with Francesca, unwiring herself.
I hadn't picked a horse, but I'd back her,
all the way!

French Rhythm

brass and woodwind float Rues – summer breezes –
hinge in places and squares –
French speak a rhythm and combines as one –
the trombone slurs a triple apostrophe –
the trumpet emphasises words started –
the saxophone nods its trunk of expression –
the clarinet stutters a background of exuberance –
the double bass reaches deep in heavy dreaming –
the French horn stumbles a pendulum of timing.

Hail

hail in spring on pavement
dances transparent rhythm
a sparkle of silver see-through
urgent its fall from strata layers
to urban's edge and kerb
formed to congealed mass
before the meltdown begins

Hans Heysen

Droving into the light

through the pillared trunks
there's entrance here, sunlight beyond,
unlike the columns of cathedral
crafted stone hand-laid
to pulpits and altars
the sifted light on leadlight colours.

here, broken gums, great torsos of time
stand their ground
lashed by seasons' storms
branches ripped form,
and the amputee of hollow
bark bleeding crusted folds

but always new skins reflecting light
hope to those early settlers,
harsh southern hemisphere's glare
that squints our heritage, our familiarity
to a land we love

Overkill

paramilitarised, jumpsuited and masked
helmeted for a most difficult task,

forlorn, perplexed he stood
and over his head a trackie hood

they were ten in masculine gender,
no chance now of his bewildered surrender

moving closer now, and black all around
like a rabbit he dashed,
shoulders close to the ground
till a repetition of shots
a deafening sound

free at last he hid away then
left behind those overdressed ten

they called up their hummers
and disengaged their guns
but alas they were
too overdressed to get in.

Overpassed

the coat hanger of overpass stretched
                        over freeway's rush
slung from the wardrobes of winter cloud,
and the Hume an hour out of Melbourne
                        was gathering speed,
  long lines of b-doubles positioning
                        for the hills ahead,
    overnight buses changing gears
                        waking their sleep
and cars winding through to the magnet
                        of city's commercial call,
a sign in rough print hung as lone washing
                        overpassing them,
    causing their upward glance
    a cut out from wool bale's side
                        frayed at fibres' edge
and splashed with rough hands' caress
                        it read

        'Julie
       come home
       I love you.'
a change from the speed and directional signs
  more poignant to every day direction
                        crossroads that lead apart,
and Julie, was she a nurse, a secretary, a teacher
was she before children, with children, after children,
    did she travel each day, freeway's way,
      her steely determination
                      not to look up.

Reading at Readings

some days he would fold hours into pages
his back to the sales counter
her voice a soundtrack to his reading

some days he purchased books
he would never open
just to read her imprint again

other days bookmark his page
until words transferred images of her between

Roadkill

on a Barkly tableland, north and further south
where grasses spinifex thin to bald clay pans
edge the long roads as shooting stars fallen
steer trains on night skies
till before the bridge that funnels them in
the meteor of headlights moments before the roadkill
and kangaroos humped in death's angle
their limbs pointing early morning light
till nature cleans up, the eagle, the dingo, the crow

on a London bridge that crosses them to bars and nightclubs
a moon on the river as large coin thrown their hopes their wishes
until a truck delivering a message comes down on them
their fallen sculpture as statues smashed in religious wars
urgent the ambulance, the police, and a terrorist shot dead

Roundabout of dreams

life's journey
memories, and contemplation
that rest on small shelves
of my dreams,
at times seem mundane yet
somehow remain catalogued,
until in the stutter of nights connect
come selected through a sepia of drift
before their fade of multiply,
as sunbeams between curtains gap
or shutters that slant beams of
                morning light

and so a roundabout of dreams
interrupt my day, demand storage
                in folds of writing
unpublished between life's covers
till stored to clouds drifting sunset
until, on the round-a-bout of earth's
curvature a new day distant
              formation repeats

Searching paddocks

from a road's bend, camber leaning view
                pastures spring of colour
suddenly a mesh of fence enclosing
tapered, reaching, towering silent communication
from arms of brackets holding
dished display searching direction
           of satellites signal
virtual transfer to a digital world
Googles fast tracked from clouds storage
Facebook's libraries of flippant word
and headlines all a Twitter

further on a eucalyptus spread
in western districts extravagance
limbs holding knotted joints,
shading a huddle of sheep,
humming a whisper of warm wind
           through,
processing carbon intake,
kookaburras perched call of jokes,
and small birds flitter through
           their calm twitter

Small shelters

the shelter shed beside the oval
bare knees that quiver anticipation
the school team reserves awaiting
                their turn

the blind, its open sides allowing
                gun barrel's turn
its camouflaged roof sheltering
                camouflaged men
their war games exploding
early morning light over swamps
                reflection

the school bus shelter, boys up one end
                girls the other
until year twelve

the mountain trail shelter, lonely in emptiness
its opening opposite to prevailing winds
awaiting the idle wanderer

yesterday's golf course shelters
linked in Scottish history
sheltering a wardrobe of tartan clothes
the plus fours, and long pleated kilts

Smart Retro Bistro

dished symbols to the sounds
of inverted acoustic
and patrons bouncing their word
off concrete walls
the cold edge of formica tabled
yet somehow undressed,
a pinch of salt and pepper plated
the clipboard of menu
a table numbered, where once
was a rose

The Batsman and the Butterfly

December in Queensland
clouds drumbeat distant chorus
a monsoonal trace of war dance
rain down a coast weakening resolve
intermittent now as sparse crowds
                          seats apart
the 'Gabba', its theatre of pitch
and covers as curtain call
and program of sessions between, across three states India v Australia
stretching isolation, anticipation

one win each, a draw and one more to go
a final innings on a fifth day
India needing 362 runs to win or remain
                          at the crease for a draw
and runs came as sheep up ramps
and bails holding value, winning
their time perhaps to ride our sheep's back

and Cheteshwar Pujara, leaving balls through
blocking 140kg of hard speed that would shudder a bat,
twist the hinges of wrist, explode a hollow thump
                        through helmet's layers
and crash his caged ribs, screaming hurt,
bruised and battered, protecting a wicket
coupling a stand with other's rotating on last balls over

till after lunch, and Cummings coming,
he stepped from the crease, a gloved wave to a bowler's rage
and there a butterfly stumbled, a faltered flight
bellowed small puffs of wing
driven on warmer western winds
sheltered now, over play fields of green

and hovered on Pujara's line of ball
lost now in a camouflage of sightscreen, distant,
loping wings teasing invitation
to the spin of Lyon's imitation,
or was it perhaps of Indian girls
                         gliding sari wave, to him, past him,
away from him, their colours, the whisper of silks
there ripple of kisses, calling him home,
yet, his hesitation of runs, holding him back,
until a draw assured, and within reach
with others to make the runs
the butterfly floating away, that would tempt his bat
                         a six away,
till caught by hands enclosing,
he carried his bat to boundary's applause
the butterfly and the batsman soon to western skies
across a Simpson desert, the rock art of a Pilbara,
sunsets as sheets of sari, calling them home

Yesterday's news

those broad sheets that held our arms,
layout that framed the ink on midnight's
                        time line,
turning a page as mainsail in urgent about
                        on yesterday's news,
sheets from conveyor line finding a crease
                        exacting their fold,
bundled on trucks before morning light
                        a new day dawning,
daybreak heaped their sprawl kerbside
as paperboys skid bikes before they load,
and fifty journalists, their opinion, their investigation,
                        airborne to front yards
                           a night's work tabled, consumed

The potter and the moulder

clay
: clays compacted in silent compression
layered on ages of sleep,
insulated in suffocation of moist homogeny,
as newborn damp, from birth's placenta
until they dig in, scoop the skinless flesh
below earth's crust,
packed to plastic bags, and opened to potter's hands
massages, caresses, palms a flare
draws the hollow of pot, extends shape,
the turn of wheel
fires a glaze that brings it to life.

the potter
: extension draws her day, her reach
as late shafts of afternoon sun
stretch her silhouette of shadow
her hollow of back and shoulder
turning inspection
her arms in slender wave
and fingers working shape
on revolve of hollowed vase
the flute of rim full as kisses

the glaze
: the bone white of ceramic
until the glaze of resurrection
of sunrise peeping colour
of sunset's promised endurance
till moonlight's reflection
the glaze as ochre from oven's
claypan
the reds and mauves as lava's flow

The Pull

kite
      at 10 holding the arch of nylon string skywards
      a father behind me now, after the launch
     his spider legs and arms along a beach,
    'Hold on tight, I'll keep you down if you're lifted',
   this sudden pull on life, those unseen currents
  and a physical telepathy down line that tugs fight

squid
       hand lines trail the drift of boat, and him
      standing in the up and down of wave
    arms in slow motion flail, jig a lure beneath,
 till one tightens, cuts through the swell, pulls back,
tugging on transparent wings, hidden in depths of fight
 then breaking a surface, exhaling stored camouflage
  as oil spill, a liquid ash offered to a new world
   tentacles meshed in the manufactured iridescence
      of lure holding its devil grip

sleeping
      her pull of sheets rolling away from him
               cocooning urgent privacy
    holding as anchor from drift   away
          from life's ebb and flow
  and dreams that once included her form
  her turn of shoulder that slow-motioned
             her toss of hair
 her shape as geometry but rounded to curve
till lost in the mathematics of chance.

end
    tubes that connected him, limp the pump of flow,
      of oxygen's pull through, lifting his frail frame
        a comb pulling waves though thin hair
    and gentle tugs of hands holding his, willing his
          holding on

The seatbelt

and miles earlier, before the mandatory clip
as father's braces hanging from door
awaiting the finesse of adjustment
that somehow never quite fitted

until the statistic of crash, and our roll over
of acceptance
until design moulded our seats
and belts slided direction
holding us in comfortable connection

The Sideways Kick

better known as the Banana, or Boomerang Kick

the Rioli of bananas bunched, curved,
their mob from shoulders of others
        and a ball that will bend
        its track through

and Betts, from a boundary marked
he stands facing centre circle
his dreaming perhaps of waterhole centred
and the rewards that will come
a direction return as boomerang will

and Goodes, his war dance to boundaries
        of distance between
his elbow bend the shadow of boomerang
the spectator mob over fence's divide
        from racist's call
and from a boundary the curve of kick
        adding score

'Brisbane Lions', and coastal slope of 'Gold Finger',
of sorting, of manipulation,
until packed for selection interstate
a new breed from further north
green and smooth their innocence of youth
before the ripening of experience
the peeling back their curve of skills
barefoot, 'before the boots come on'.

Urban Highs and Lows

once a valley of urbane network
its spokes of laneway from urban hub
boulevards as armies wide
sweeping bends to
monuments, muscling in

and now the 'high rise'
gathered in their pods of zoning
reaching as models, cloned, anorexic,
to that catwalk in the sky

Van Gogh Exhibition

trees as gnarled arthritic,
their lean of crippled trunk
hinging branch's muscle of knot,
drifts of snow as sheets
tossed in hospital layers,
and sleet in frozen winds
holding sepia shadows to
a shade cloth sky,

until a season's change,
his autumn, summer and spring release
southern France and The Hills of St Remy
and Pine Trees at Sunset,
grasses magnified to winds adjustment
tossed in relentless adoration
bowing to sun's summer warmth
till wildflowers' fragrant explosion
on a background of violet wafered
in season's compression,
as autumn leaves fall so too his ear
severed, diluting his inner voices
as gentle rain does

Words Meeting

words evolve through a spontaneity of thought
                                    join a verbal continuity
its spiel smooth before emphasis
                        of fade to pause

a written word needs a home
a book, a pad, a folder
holding between

a writers group needs a venue
audio assistance and critique
our word is our group
and here we are between new covers
at the Peppermill

Writers Festival, Adelaide 2018

from a northern terrace
tumbling towards a river Torrens
us gathered east and west on pods of festival
hanging shade beneath elms' expanse
in Adelaide's march of summer heat
words come fallen yet honed
as free fall of autumn leaves
that will glide a landing
the writer the presenter reaching enthusiasm
as though there's more to this story
than the book might portray
her library of audience
and us as books shelved
content as pages feathered

Yesterday's cars

Holden's HD, Ford's Falcon and Valiant's Charge
my first car a Morris 840, its hooded folds in open summer
telepathy of gear change, and steering curve
to the routine of destination between saw tooth
of factory's roofs delivery apprentice to his
learning habits,
and at the Frankston Drive-in with Liz
stars reflected that blanked us in
and my car resting us.

About this ageing vessel

Administration and Admission

airports that blanket a sky
confuse commuter
their allocation of seats away
and luggage to other lands,
and hospitals too,
that number our warded beds
our luggage reduced to pyjamas
and gown
patient in shuffled queues
or slide from ambulance bed,
I asked a return ticket
confused they told me,
'there's no return'.

Any time soon

an old man's lament

to travel some space
drift through cloud
without the spear of jet,
rather to linger, hover,
the shape of cumulus
morph their jovial shift
as old friends around
and further out
slim streaks of strata
as platforms of judgement
temptation of vapour's caress
any time soon

Floors

always the floors,
their space of vinyl reaching,
her life trodden by others
to transfer shine to their souls,
her Italian migration to 'Fords'
                cafeteria,
and workers from same countries
the buff of her revolve of machine
circling her resolve to mirror finish
equal she thought to the duco
of Falcons, and Fairlanes
down the line
and later a husband
his boots from the engine foundry
stamping his love for her

after children, her floors at home,
then with other grandmothers
their mops a swish to local gossip
the routine of hospital and
rounds of warded floors,
of passages that will trolley others
away in the dead of the night

Foghorn and Ultrasound

the foghorn sounded intermittent wakening
before ultrasound that would probe my day,
press its hunch of lenses around my stomach
                         imaging within,
    a bladder and kidneys either side,
fluid retention, polyps, tumours, exposed
as CCTV cameras do to others on street corners
    the narrow passages of urban function,
    me, ultra-intimidated, through clouds
        to a urologist's computer.

Footsteps

steps on pavement as unwritten word
imprints impression reflecting,
unseen to soul's direction
the click of heels unrecorded,
now the slur of shuffle
tuned to city's static
to a swale of distant curve
uphill downhill his earthly interaction
laneways graffiti crowding, stop, start, stare,
past doorways where others lean anonymous
his rooms of parallel boards, in hollow wait
his footstep causing a welcome squeak
a groan at the monotony of daily routine

In Confined Urgency

from the artery of main road to the capillary of suburban street
        a siren's flash of silence,
           searching street numbers in morning sun,
her wave from a driveway and neighbours their focus from the edge of curtain
their horizontal adjustment of louvres that squints a view of paramedics
        loaded with life support through a front door
          and the privacy of his floors and ceilings
beside him now defibrillator and leads from pads searching a rhythm a beat
along life's road
        the artery
the capillary
his direction ahead.

It's Inconclusive

it's inconclusive, undecided, unconforming,
the test, the X-ray, the colour,
as the old moonah, its trunk along the ground
in exhausted sleep, yet growing,
as a window cracked yet holding against wind
its crooked line winking see-through,
as first love, inconclusive, undecided
                          until the first kiss,
unconforming to individual trial
                          but lasting.

Night Decks

decks reach to rails and dark sea below
further out a line of night sky bedded down
stars climb horizon's arch, umbrella us,
and moon traces a Kimberley coast
that floats our dreams,
romances our distances between.
alas a cruise floating nautical miles away
and us flying home to southern skies
a fallen star to nature's call, urgent.

between tests, waiting the jam
of hospital schedule
now my back deck harbours me
the warmth of sun its light opening
my page
the sound of winter waves surfing
sand dunes
by night my visits timed to a lighthouse
searching light
its boards cool to bare feet
and southern skies pointing direction
my flow slowed, caught in the twinkle
of starlight

Night passage

he walked those lonely corridors at night
(avoiding other's mid-morning shuffle
and talk of doctor's orders)

past wards of charts measuring
life's ups and downs
nurse's station reduced to a
night's breath
the horizontal of ghost sheathed
in white
not floating but trolleyed away
through plastic doors

Old Shadows

shadows of themselves once,
as old wallpapers loosened
their fade in rooms familiar,
on the curve of life's spine
they shuffle from sitting
through doors that frame them,
to backyard walls and winter's sun
spotlighting transparency,
their waxed mâché as puppets
exaggerated features and clothing
                          that hangs,
their menu of life
a scone and cup of tea, by day,
a cup of soup at night
but in a different cup

Red

red dust of Oodnadatta trailed thin
followed us around the edge of Simpson
laid foundation for camp mattress
shared variation of red on sunset backdrop
framed the yellow of dingoes
on distant ridge
red wine and rose pink poured to fading light
reflected our day, a blowout near Maree
a battery flat from exhaustion
the up and down of tent
and pack rack stacked,
the red in my urine, unexpected
gentle to the red dust of native land,
that would shut me down
till eventually between wings
on the red kangaroo
above red deserts dream
and home to hospital

The Curtain Pull

the routine around my warded bed, sunlight at the edge of window
and memories of sunbeams that trailed to the end of my childhood bed,
visitors to other beds and conversation familiar to those that visit me
    until the curtain pull that envelopes me,
        screens a routine of privacy,
        closes my day,
        isolates my thoughts to unowned reality.

The Food Tray

its rectangular dimension harbours small containers,
plastic with lids
that peel inner ingredients; fruit juice, yoghurt, butter, dessert, all wait their turn.
'Ah' but first to lift the domed lid, upturned and left on blanket's edge
and there as if robotically served, fish, peas, mash, pumpkin.
I tear the folds that envelop
        a knife,
        fork,
        the pepper and salt.

Acknowledgements

Roundabout
A comma here, a spell-check there.
Repositioning my work yet maintaining a rhythm as walking on through,
but in-step.

I'm very grateful to Marion Higgins and Martin Smith of Seaside Scribes, Queenscliff for their guidance in editing and collating these pieces into this collection, *Roundabout*.

About the Author

Roger Furphy was born in Shepparton, Victoria, in 1940. He is a retired foundry man caught with a name depicting rumour and exaggeration. This gives him an opportunity perhaps to write prose as loose yarn, and poetry free that may reduce the stretch of Aussie parochialism, bend the elasticity of do-good words.

www.ingramcontent.com/pod-product-compliance
Lightning Source LLC
Chambersburg PA
CBHW070951080526
44587CB00015B/2267